A SERIOUS CALL
TO HOLY LIVING

LIVING CLASSICS
WILLIAM LAW

A SERIOUS CALL TO HOLY LIVING

6189

A Contemporary Version by
Marvin D. Hinten

Tyndale House Publishers, Inc.
Wheaton, Illinois

William Law's original work was first published in 1728 under the title *A Serious Call to a Devout and Holy Life.*

All Bible quotations are taken from the King James (Authorized) Version.

First printing, April 1985

Library of Congress Catalog Card Number 84-52224
ISBN 0-8423-5861-7, paper
Copyright 1985 by Marvin D. Hinten
All rights reserved
Printed in the United States of America

CONTENTS

THE LIFE OF WILLIAM LAW

William Law was born in England in 1686. After attending Emmanuel College, Cambridge, he was ordained as an Anglican clergyman in 1711 and continued at Cambridge with a fellowship. In 1716 he was forced to leave both the ministry and the university for refusing to take the oaths of allegiance to George I, the new king and head of the Church of England.

Edward Gibbon, grandfather of the author of *The Decline and Fall of the Roman Empire*, hired Law in 1723 as a tutor for his son (the historian's father). During that time, Law produced his two greatest works—*On Christian Perfection* (1726) and *A Serious Call to a Devout and Holy Life* (1729).

In 1740 he left the Gibbon household and retired to King's Cliffe—his birthplace—where he had inherited a small property from his father. Law devoted himself to prayer and good works until his death in 1761.

INTRODUCTION

Just as *A Serious Call to a Devout and Holy Life* influenced
two notable eighteenth-century Christians, John Wesley
and Samuel Johnson, it has influenced Christians of our
own time, such as C. S. Lewis and Elton Trueblood. It is, in
other words, a timeless book.

But though ideas may be timeless, language is not. Eighteenth-century diction and style have pushed Law's book
into undeserving obscurity. Perhaps the most unfortunate
feature of his style is simply bulk. The unabridged *Serious
Call* contains over 130,000 words.

This edition contains 20,000 words. It is a distillation of
Law; an essence, rather than a scholarly work. My purpose
in abridging and paraphrasing Law's work is to provide a
stimulating spur to contemporary devotion. Therefore,
Law's examples are updated (carriages, for instance, become cars) and his sections on now-irrelevant problems are
omitted.

But only the illustrations and diction are modernized; in
condensing and restating William Law's thoughts, I have
not substituted my own. Thus, when Law claims in this
edition that girls might well outdo boys in science and

public speaking (Chapter 19), I am not arbitrarily imposing twentieth-century feminism on his ideas. (The original says that if girls were allowed to compete with boys, in "arts and sciences, of learning and eloquence . . . I have much suspicion they would often prove our superiors.") Law was hardly a feminist in the modern sense; but as this example indicates, he was not just a product of his times, either.

There are elements in *A Serious Call* with which we will disagree. But it encourages us to take God seriously, to try to please him. In Chapter 3 Law says, "We cannot offer to God the service of angels; we cannot obey him as humanity in a state of perfection could; but fallen men *can* do their best."

May this book encourage you to do your best.

—Marvin D. Hinten

CHAPTER ONE
THE MEASURE OF CHRISTIAN LIFE

DEVOTION is neither public nor private prayer; all prayers are mere instances of devotion. True devotion signifies a life given to God. A devout person, therefore, is one who lives no longer to his own will or to the way of the world, but to the sole will of God—one who considers God in everything, serves God in everything, and does everything to his glory.

God alone is to be the measure of our prayers. In them we look wholly to him. We are only to pray in ways and for things that are suitable to his glory.

As we make God the measure of our prayers, we should also make him the measure of our lives. Thus any use of talents, time, or money that is not strictly according to God's will is a miserable failure. We fill our prayers with wisdom and holiness in order to fill our lives with the same. Thoughtless ways of life are as absurd as thoughtless prayers.

Since people seldom consider this, we often see a strange mixture in their lives. They are strict about attending Sunday worship, but when a church service is over, they are just like those who never come. In their ways of spending time and money—their cares and entertainments—they are indistinguishable from the rest of the world.

Take Julius,* for example. Though he wouldn't dare to miss church, he lives the rest of his life by whim. Yet the whole tenor of Scripture opposes an idle, careless life as much as it stands against gluttony and drunkenness.

If a woman were to tell Julius that he could freely neglect church services, Julius would consider her unchristian. But if she were to say that he should enjoy himself exactly as others do, spending his time and money like others of his economic level, Julius would never suspect her of blasphemy and false teaching. If Julius were to read the New Testament from beginning to end, however, he would find this course of life condemned on every page.

We would doubt the spiritual depth of a person who claims to lead the Christian life without prayer. But to ignore our own use of time and money is as foolish as ignoring prayer. And to spend our lives in ways that we cannot (or do not) offer to God is as foolish as making up prayers without offering them to God.

Christianity prescribes guidelines to govern the ordinary actions of our lives. Thus to follow those guidelines is just as important as to worship God. Christianity teaches us how to eat and drink; how to use our time and money; how to behave toward the sick, poor, and old; whom to particularly love and esteem; how to treat our enemies; and how to deny ourselves. Each of these aspects of the faith is as important as worship.

The Gospels never prescribe public worship; it is perhaps

*All persons in *A Serious Call* are imaginary, invented by Law to illustrate his points. In many cases the characters' names themselves have meanings which further enhance Law's illustrations. Here, for example, "Julius" was chosen as the name of a worldly Christian. The suggestion is that (Julius) Caesar is the worldly power as opposed to God.

the duty least insisted upon in Scripture. Frequent attendance at worship is nowhere commanded in all the New
Testament. On the other hand, the devotion that should
govern the ordinary actions of our lives is found in almost
every verse of Scripture. Jesus and his apostles are wholly
taken up in doctrines that relate to the common life. They
call us to reject the world and to differ in every way from its
spirit; to reject the world's goods and to fear none of its
evils; to live as pilgrims in spiritual watching, holy fear, and
heavenly aspiration; and to take up our daily crosses, deny-
ing ourselves.

They teach us to seek blessed mourning and spiritual
poverty; to forsake the vanity of riches; to not worry about
the future; to live in profound humility; and to rejoice in
worldly suffering. Furthermore, we are to reject lust, greed,
and pride; to forgive and bless our enemies; to love mankind as God does; to give up our whole hearts and affections to God; and to strive to enter through the narrow gate
into a life of eternal glory.

This is what our blessed Savior taught as devotion. Isn't it
strange, then, that people place so much emphasis upon
attendance at public worship and so little on these daily
duties commanded in every page of the Gospels?

If we are to hold contempt for the world and affection for
heaven, these things must appear consistently throughout
our lives. If self-denial is a condition of salvation, all of us
who would be saved must make it part of our everyday
lives. If contentment and thankfulness are duties to God,
they are duties in every circumstance. If we are to be new
creatures in Christ, we must also demonstrate new ways of
living.

Thus it is with all Christian virtues; they are not ours
unless they are ours daily. Christianity does not allow us to
live in the common manner, conforming to fads and indulg-

ing ourselves. We must live above and contrary to the world. If our lives are not daily courses of humility, self-denial, and heavenly affection, we are not living the Christian life.

But this concept is alien to most churchgoers. We see these people nicely dressed, singing hymns, and enjoying fine preachers in polite company. If we look into their lives, though, we see them to be the same sort of people as those who do not worship. The only differences between them are differences of taste or personality. Both have the same worldly cares, fears, and joys; they have the same life-styles and mind-set. In each we see the same fondness for nice housing and cars, the same vanity for attractive clothing, the same self-love and indulgence, the same fondness for entertainment, and the same trifling conversations.

I am not comparing these "good Christian people" with thieves or prostitutes, but with moral non-Christians. Consider two moral men. Leo is good-natured, generous, and truthful. In religious matters, however, he hardly knows the difference between a Christian and a Buddhist.

Hubert, on the other hand, was raised a Christian. He buys Christian books and records. He knows the "true meaning of Christmas" and honors all the big-name Christians. He doesn't drink or smoke, is honest and truthful, and speaks of religion as an important concern. Hubert has religion enough to be considered by the world (and by himself) as a Christian, while Leo is far from religion. But let us consider their relationship to the world. In that respect, we will find Hubert and Leo very much alike—seeking, using, and enjoying all that can be gotten in this world, and for the same reasons. We will find that prosperity, pleasure, success, and recognition are just as much the sources of happiness for Hubert as for Leo. But if Christianity has not changed a man's mind in relation to these things, what can we say it has done for him?

Jesus said, "Take no thought, saying, What shall we eat? or, What shall we drink? or, Wherewithal shall we be clothed? (For after all these things do the Gentiles seek)" (Matt. 6:31-32). If to be thus concerned with necessary things shows we are not yet of a Christian spirit, surely to be like the world in our concern for pleasure indicates we are merely adding Christian devotion to a heathen life.

CHAPTER TWO
GOOD INTENTIONS

WHY are the lives of many churchgoers so strangely contrary to the principles of Christianity? Simply because people do not have the intention to please God in all their actions.

It was this intention that made the early Christians such fine examples of piety. And if we stop and ask ourselves why we are not as holy as the early Christians were, our hearts will tell us it is not due to inability, but simply because we never really intended it. We observe Sunday worship because we intend to do so. When we intend to please God in our other actions, we will be able to do so.

Let a clergyman cultivate such intention, and he will converse as if he has been brought up by an apostle. He will no longer daydream about promotions and fame. He will no longer complain about having a small church or a small car.

Let a businessman have this intention, and it will make him a saint in his shop. His everyday business will be a course of wise actions made holy to God. He will consider not just what methods make him richest, but which will make his business most acceptable to God.

Again, let the wealthy man have this intention. He cannot now live as he fancies. He cannot live in idleness, indulgence, and pleasure, because these things cannot be turned into means of holiness. He will not ask whether God will forgive the vanity of his expenses and the careless consumption of his time, but he will seek to discover whether God is pleased with his life. He will not look at the lives of others to determine how he ought to spend his income, but will instead look into the Scriptures and take to heart every instruction for rich men.

With such an intention, the wealthy Christian will have nothing to do with expensive clothing, for the condemned rich man in the Gospel was clothed with fine linen. He will deny himself personal indulgences, for our blessed Savior says, "Woe unto you that are rich! for ye have received your consolation" (Luke 6:24).

You may argue that dressing nicely is your only weakness, so it doesn't really matter. But that is like a person saying, "Except for occasionally burglarizing homes, I lead a good life." To comfort themselves about their use of fine clothing and accessories, people often look for someone who carries the matter "too far." A woman who uses little makeup may condemn a woman who uses much, yet their motivations and attitudes about makeup may be the same.

How is it possible for a man who intends to please God financially to bury his money in finery? This is just as impossible as a person who intends to please God with his words, then meets other people with swearing and lying. All wasting and unreasonable spending are done deliberately.

I have chosen to explain the problem of unholy living by appealing to intention, for it makes the case so plain. It is easy for an employee to know whether he intends to please his employer in all his actions. Likewise, a Christian can certainly know if he intends to please God with his life.

Consider two people; one prays regularly and the other doesn't. The difference between them is not that one has the physical strength required to pray and the other doesn't. The difference is simply that one intends to please God by praying, and the other one doesn't.

One person throws away his time and money on useless diversions. Another person is careful of every hour and uses his money for charity. The difference is not that one has power over his time and money and the other doesn't; it is that one desires to please God, and the other one doesn't.

The problem of unholy living does not stem from the fact that we desire to use money and time wisely, but fail due to the weaknesses of human nature. The problem is that we do not *intend* to be as responsible and devout as we can.

I do not mean to suggest that human intention can take the place of divine grace. Nor do I mean to say that through pure intention we can make ourselves perfect. I am simply saying that lack of desire to please God causes irregularities that by grace we should have the power to avoid.

CHAPTER THREE
STRIVING FOR SALVATION

IN his goodness and mercy God forgives our weaknesses and lapses. We have no reason, however, to expect the same mercy for those sins we live in because we choose to.

For instance, perhaps you have made little progress in acquiring the most important Christian virtues. You shrug off this lack of progress as inevitable: after all, you say, everyone falls far short of perfection. But that is not the point. The question is not whether perfection can be attained, but whether you come as near to it as sincere intention and diligence can carry you. Only when you have carried out the Christian life with your best efforts may you justly hope that your imperfections will not be held against you.

The salvation of our souls is set forth in Scripture as a thing of diligence that is to be worked out with fear and trembling. We are told that "strait is the gate, and narrow is the way, which leadeth unto life, and few there be that find it" (Matt. 7:14). We are also told that "many are called, but few are chosen" (Matt. 22:14). And apparently many who have taken pains to obtain their salvation will miss it: "Strive to enter in at the strait gate: for many, I say unto you, will seek to enter in, and shall not be able" (Luke 13:24).

Christianity is a state of striving. Many will fall short of their salvation because they didn't care or take enough action.

Therefore, every Christian should examine his life by these teachings. They are plain marks of our condition. If salvation is given only to those who strive for it, it seems reasonable to me to consider whether we are indeed striving for it.

Suppose my religion is only a formal compliance with the accepted form of worship in my area. Suppose that it costs me no pain or trouble; it puts me under no restraints; I have no careful thoughts or sober reflections about it. Isn't it careless to think that I am striving to enter in at the narrow gate?

If I am spending my time and fortune primarily for pleasure, and am a stranger to prayer and self-denial, then how can it be said that I am working out my salvation in fear and trembling? If I seek worldly enjoyments as most people do, why should I think I am among the few who are walking the narrow path to heaven?

The Bible makes it plain that salvation corresponds with a sincere effort to obtain it. Imperfect people will be received as having pleased God—in spite of their defects—if they have done their utmost to try to please him.

Of course, we cannot offer to God the service of angels; we cannot obey him as we could were we perfect. But fallen men can do their best. If we stop short of our best, for all we know we may be stopping short of the mercy of God, for God has not promised mercy to the negligent.

These truths should not fill our minds with anxiety. Rather, they should excite us to zealously seek Christian perfection. The best way for anyone to know how much he ought to strive for holiness is to ask himself what will make him comfortable at the hour of death. Anyone who seriously asks himself this question will answer that at death he would wish to have been as holy as he possibly could.

Penitens was a prosperous businessman who died at age thirty-five. Shortly before his death some neighbors visited him, and he said to them, "Friends, I know your thoughts. You think how sad it is to see such a prosperous young man dying. Had I visited any of you in this condition, I would have probably thought the same.

"But now my thoughts are considerably different from yours. It is not troubling to me now to think about dying young or before my business is fully established. In a few hours I will be buried; then I'll find myself either forever happy in God's favor or eternally separated from all peace. Can any words sufficiently express the littleness of everything else?

"We consider death as a miserable separation from the enjoyments of life. Yet what is there miserable or dreadful about death besides the consequences of it? When a man is dead, what matters to him except the state he is then in?

"Our friend Larry, as you know, died while dressing for a party. Do you think he is now distressed that he didn't get to live until the party was over?

"If I am now going into the joys of God, do you think it grieves me that I do not have time to make a few more business deals? And if I am to join the lost souls, do you think I would be happier joining them as a wealthy old man?

"When you are as near death as I am, you will know that age, wealth, and status mean as little as whether the apartment in which you are dying is well-furnished. If I now owned a thousand worlds, I would exchange them all for one year of devotion and good works.

"You may be surprised to see me so full of remorse when I have belonged to the church and lived free of scandal. But what a poor thing it is to say only that I have not committed murder or adultery. Yet that is all I can say of myself.

"In my business I have been prudent and methodical. I have studied books and gladly conversed with people of experience and judgment. Why didn't I bring these attributes to Christianity? Had I only my frailties and imperfections to lament at this time, I would lie here humbly trusting in the mercies of God. But how can I call a thorough neglect of religious improvement a frailty or imperfection?"

At this point Penitens was stopped by a convulsion. He never spoke again.

CHAPTER FOUR
GAINFUL EMPLOYMENT

PEOPLE will differ in their choices of employment, but offering up to God a pure heart as a daily sacrifice is the common business of all. Therefore the rich should not gratify themselves nor the poor vex themselves—all must turn their labor into continual spiritual service.

In order to make our employment an acceptable service to God, we must engage in it as if it were a work of charity or piety. "Whether therefore ye eat, or drink, or whatsoever ye do, do all to the glory of God" (1 Cor. 10:31). Our employment, then, must glorify God just as our prayers do. If a person pursues his business simply to raise his income and status, he is no longer serving God in his employment. Vain and earthly desires are no more allowable in our employment than in our prayers.

Most types of employment are acceptable for Christians. But they should not take up all of our strength, thoughts, and time. No human business is as great or important as spiritual development and nurture. After all, the Scriptures represent this life and the greatest things in it as vapors, dreams, and shadows.

A businessman may justly think it is God's will for him to

support himself and others by selling things. But if his chief end in business is to grow rich and retire in luxury, his business loses its innocence. Such a person lives no more to the glory of God than a person who gambles to achieve the same end. In the same way charity and fine clothing seem to be quite different. But if a person is charitable for the same reason another person dresses well (in order to be noticed and admired), there is really no difference in the actions.

A greedy or ambitious businessman might say, to excuse himself, that his business dealings are acceptable because he only deals in lawful items. But a glutton could similarly excuse himself by saying he only eats lawful foods. A Christian is required not only to be honest, but to be of a Christian spirit in all things, and to make his life an exercise of repentance, humility, and heavenly affection. This includes his business life.

It is clear that a Christian should enter no further into business than he can offer to God as a reasonable service. For Christ has redeemed us only that we should live to the glory of God. Without this basic motivation, the most lawful employment becomes sinful.

A man is not considered honest because he is fair and just to some people or upon several occasions, but because honesty is the measure of all his dealings with everybody. Such is the case with humility. It must be the ruling habit of our minds, applying itself to business and to all our plans and actions, before it can truly be called a part of us.

Therefore we must be honest, humble, and devoted not only in particular instances, but in every aspect of our lives, remaining steadfast even against opposition. The more we pay for any truth, the better the bargain. Our integrity becomes a pearl only when we have parted with all to keep it.

CHAPTER FIVE
RESPONSIBILITY IN RETIREMENT

THOSE who are comfortably retired or independently wealthy often have vast amounts of time and fortunes at their command. Their freedom lays on them a great responsibility to choose and do the best things. Much will be required of them, for much has been given them.

If you are in this state, without a boss to serve, serve your own soul. Nourish it with good works, give it peace in solitude, strengthen it with prayer, make it wise with reading, enlighten it with meditation, tender it with love, sweeten it with humility, humble it with penance, enliven it with psalms and hymns, and comfort it with frequent reflections upon future glory. Teach it to imitate those angels who, though they attend human events, "always behold the face of my Father which is in heaven" (Matt. 18:10).

Every person's circumstances are bestowed upon him by God. We must therefore use every situation for him. When people spend a little time in prayer and then waste the rest, or give 10 percent of their money to church then squander the rest, they have not considered the nature of Christianity. If it is desirable to be heavenly minded at church, then it is always desirable.

If someone would prove to me that we do not have to always live for God, I could prove to him that we do not have to live for God at all. A person who believes in part-time Christianity may as well believe in part-time intelligence. And when we consider that belief in Christianity perfects us, raises us to God, and exalts our best side, who would wish to ever be free of it?

Thus when we are seeking to understand how a Christian ought to live, we must look to the highest precepts of the New Testament, we must examine ourselves by the spirit of Christ, we must think how the wisest people in the world have lived, we must think what degree of holiness we would wish for when leaving the world.

I have not overstated the matter. In fact, I am just complying with Paul's advice where he says, "Whatsoever things are true, whatsoever things are honest, whatsoever things are just, whatsoever things are pure, whatsoever things are lovely, whatsoever things are of good report; if there be any virtue, and if there be any praise, think on these things" (Phil. 4:8).

CHAPTER SIX
SPENDING MONEY

OUR money is just as much a gift from God as are our eyes or hands. We have no more right to squander it away than to put out our eyes or throw away our hands.

The way we use money reveals much about our character and priorities. If we waste it, we do not waste a trifle; we waste something that could be eyes to the blind, a husband to the widow, a father to the orphan. We waste that which could not only minister comfort to those in distress, but could also lay up treasure for us in heaven. So if we part foolishly with our money, we not only part with a way of comforting our fellow creatures but with a way of making ourselves eternally blessed.

Suppose a person has a stock of extra eyes and hands that he can give to anyone who lacks them. But instead of giving them to the blind and lame, he locks them up in a chest or plays with them like toys. Would we not consider him an inhuman wretch? Suppose that he is promised an eternal reward for giving away the eyes and hands, but instead he uses them to decorate his house. Would we not consider him completely insane?

Money can have much the same nature as hands and eyes. If we hoard money or waste it while the poor lack necessities, if we use it for extra clothing while some people have almost nothing to wear, aren't we near the cruelty of the person who decorated his home with hands and eyes? If we indulge ourselves in useless, expensive enjoyments rather than gaining an eternal reward for wise use of money, aren't we plagued with the insanity of the person who played with spare hands and eyes?

Buying unnecessary luxuries lowers us. Those superfluous things are like weights on our minds that make us less interested in raising our thoughts and affections to things above. Thus when we squander money we keep it from the poor to buy poison for ourselves.

> When the Son of man shall come in his glory, and all the holy angels with him, then shall he sit upon the throne of his glory: and before him shall be gathered all nations: and he shall separate them one from another, as a shepherd divideth his sheep from the goats: and he shall set the sheep on his right hand, but the goats on the left. Then shall the King say unto them on his right hand, Come, ye blessed of my Father, inherit the kingdom prepared for you from the foundation of the world: For I was an hungred, and ye gave me meat: I was thirsty, and ye gave me drink: I was a stranger and ye took me in: Naked, and ye clothed me: I was sick, and ye visited me: I was in prison, and ye came unto me. Then shall the righteous answer him, saying, Lord, when saw we thee an hungred, and fed thee? or thirsty, and gave thee drink? When saw we thee a stranger, and took thee in? or naked, and clothed thee? Or when saw we thee sick, or in prison, and came unto thee? And the King shall answer and say unto them, Verily I say unto you, Inasmuch as ye have done it unto one of the least of these my brethren, ye have done it unto me. Then shall he say also unto them on the left hand, Depart from me, ye cursed, into everlasting fire, prepared for the devil and his angels: For I was an hungred, and ye gave me no meat: I was thirsty, and ye gave me no drink: I was a stranger, and ye took me not in: naked, and ye clothed me not: sick, and in

prison, and yet visited me not. Then shall they also answer him, saying, Lord when saw we thee an hungred, or athirst, or a stranger, or naked, or sick, or in prison, and did not minister unto thee? Then shall he answer them, saying, Verily I say unto you, Inasmuch as ye did it not to one of the least of these, ye did it not to me. And these shall go away into everlasting punishment: but the righteous into life eternal.

—Matthew 25:31-46

I have quoted this passage at length because one would hardly think most Christians had ever read it. What in their lives demonstrates their belief that their salvation depends on these works? Yet the necessity of good works is asserted here in the strongest manner.

We must conclude from this passage that on the last day people who neglect these good works will be placed on the left hand and banished. There seems, therefore, no salvation apart from these good works. Yet who can be said to have done these? A person who once assisted a prisoner or relieved the poor? That would be as absurd as labeling a person "prayerful" who has said one prayer in his life.

Our Savior said, "If [someone] trespass against thee seven times in a day, and seven times in a day turn again to thee, saying, I repent; thou shalt forgive him" (Luke 17:4). If, therefore, a man ceases to forgive his brother because he has forgiven him already (or has forgiven several others), he is breaking the law of Christ concerning forgiveness.

The rule of forgiving is also the rule of giving. We are not to cease from giving because we have often given to the same person or to others. We are as obliged to continue relieving them as when we did it the first time. If we are unable to give, of course, we are under no obligation. If we can only occasionally give, then we should give occasionally; if we regularly have money to give, we ought to give regularly.

CHAPTER SEVEN
CASUAL CHRISTIANITY

MANY people live with the precepts of Christianity in their heads, but with something else in their hearts. Thus they live from year to year as mere admirers of piety.

Flavia is well off financially. She takes communion and attends church. When she hears a sermon on charity, she thinks it is a proper subject and one that people need to be reminded of. She doesn't apply it to herself, however, remembering that she gave just a few months ago.

As for people on welfare and unemployment, she knows they are all cheats and liars and will say anything to get relief. It would be a sin, she reasons, to encourage poor people in their evil ways. You would think Flavia had the tenderest conscience in the world if you could hear her talk on the danger of improper giving.

She has every attractive home furnishing and every modern appliance. She takes every opportunity for entertainment. Suppose Flavia lives ten more years. Of her thirty independent years, she will have spent fifteen in bed (she sleeps late, since no job forces her to get up). Of the remaining fifteen, fourteen or more will have been spent in eating, drinking, dressing, reading romances, watching television, listening to the stereo, and idly chatting with friends and neighbors.

I certainly won't take it upon myself to say that it's impossible for Flavia to be saved, but this much can be said: she has no scriptural grounds to think she is saved. For her whole life is in direct opposition to what the New Testament displays as evidence of a saved life.

If you would hear Flavia say she has lived like Anna the prophetess, who "served God with fastings and prayers night and day" (Luke 2:37), you would call her a liar. But is this a bigger lie than for her to claim she strove to enter in at the straight gate?

She might as well claim she had lived with Jesus while he was on earth. Yet she could have been humble, serious, devout, a lover of good books, prayerful, charitable, and meditative despite the handicap of a sizeable fortune.

It is true that indulgence, idleness, and gossip are small faults when compared to the "great sins." But even these seemingly harmless trespasses become great sins when one considers they hinder a holy attitude.

CHAPTER EIGHT
WISELY USED MONEY

IF a person can bring any one part of his life under the control of Christianity, he has a better chance to subject the rest, for God has been introduced to his thoughts.

Now by subjection, I mean subjection to God. If a woman eats less simply to improve her figure, or stops drinking simply because she hates hangovers, she might gain control over those areas without becoming a better person. But when a person is moderate or regular in anything because of Christian self-denial—to present to God a more holy life—he possesses Christian control. Bringing one area of our lives under Christian control helps our entire subjection, because it brings God more often to our thoughts.

Suppose a person should decide that, instead of watching the news, he will spend that time praying or reading Christian books. It may seem unreasonable to expect a person to abstain from things that are admittedly not sinful. Nevertheless I feel whoever would try making such a minor change would find his mind set on higher things.

Miranda (Flavia's sister) is a reasonable Christian. She has but one reason for doing or not doing something, or for liking or not liking something, and that is the will of God.

She divides her money between herself and other people. She will not give a poor person money to use for entertainment. But neither will she spend her own money this way; Miranda thinks she should be as wise with resources as she expects a poor person to be. This is Miranda's spirit. This is how she uses the gifts of God—she is simply one of a number of people supported by her fortune, and she differs from the others only in the blessedness of giving.

Three words describe Miranda's attitude about dressing; she does it neatly, cleanly, and cheaply. She is never bored; her spare hours are opportunities to pray. She eats and drinks simply, so that every meal is an exercise in self-denial.

The New Testament is her daily study; she tests herself against the principles found there. When reading the Gospels or Epistles, she imagines she is actually listening to Jesus or the apostles speak. She receives their words as attentively as if they were speaking specifically to her.

Miranda is sometimes afraid she spends too much money on books, for she cannot resist buying practical books (by practical, naturally, she means books on holiness and the Christian life). But of all human writings, the biographies of devout saints are her greatest delight. She searches them carefully, hoping to find some principle of holy living to make her own. In fact, Miranda's head and heart are so full of wisdom and holiness that she finds it difficult to talk about any other subject. If you are around Miranda while she is speaking, you almost cannot help becoming a wiser and better person.

Miranda assists not only people she knows personally, but strangers as well. "I was a stranger, and ye took me in" (Matt. 25:35), our Savior said. Who can imitate Christ, Miranda reasons, while only assisting friends and acquaintances?

"It may be," Miranda says, "that I will sometimes give to those who do not deserve it or who will not use my money wisely. But so what? Isn't that how divine goodness works? Doesn't God make his 'sun to rise on the evil and on the good' (Matt. 5:45)? Shouldn't we imitate our Father in heaven, who 'sendeth rain on the just and the unjust' (5:45)? Shall I withhold money or food from a person because he might not be good enough to deserve it? I beg God to deal with me not according to my merit, but according to his own great goodness. Shall I use a measure against someone else which I pray to God never to use against me?

"Where has Scripture made merit the measure of charity? On the contrary, the Bible says, 'If thine enemy hunger, feed him; if he thirst, give him drink' (Rom. 12:20). This plainly teaches that we are to be kind even to those who least deserve it. For if I am to do good even to my worst enemies, surely I should do good to people I don't know.

"You may say that relieving the poor encourages them to stay on relief. The same objection could be made against forgiving our enemies—that it encourages people to hurt us. The same thoughtless accusation could even be made against God's kindness—that by pouring his blessings on both the just and the unjust, the unjust people are encouraged in their wicked ways. And the same could be said against caring for the sick—that treated people will no longer strive for health. When the love of God has filled you with compassion, you will no longer make absurd objections like these.

"Whenever you turn down an opportunity to meet the needs of a poor, old, or sick Christian, ask yourself this question: 'Do I sincerely wish this person to be a fellow-heir of glory with me?' If you'll search your soul, you'll find you really don't. It's impossible to truly wish that person the happiness of heaven while disregarding his happiness here.

"For this reason," says Miranda, "I give to whomever I can. Our Savior has said that it is more blessed to give than to receive. Actually, then, we ought to look on the needy as our friends and benefactors. They will be our advocates with God on the day of judgment. They will help us to a far greater blessedness than we are giving them."

CHAPTER NINE
TRUE WORSHIP AND THANKSGIVING

WE glorify God with psalms and hymns of thanksgiving simply because we are to glorify him in all possible ways. Verbal praises and thanksgiving, however, are not necessarily more holy in themselves than other acts.

Actions are often more significant than words. If God is to be worshipped with thanksgiving, then it's obviously higher praise to thank him in the midst of every circumstance than only to thank him in a set time at church. It is easy to worship God in church, setting aside a few Sunday hours. A greater measure of devotion is to worship him in difficult areas, such as humility and self-denial. It is better to be holy than to have holy prayers. I do not mean to downplay the value of prayers; I mean only to point out that they are a slender part of devotion, when compared to a devout life.

To see this more clearly, imagine a person who never misses church. He praises God lustily in hymns and prayers. But throughout the week he is bored, restless, and irritable. Can his songs of thanksgiving on Sunday be considered true? It is ludicrous to combine bent knees with proud thoughts, heavenly petitions with earthly treasures, and brief prayers with extended entertainments.

The Son of God did not come from above to add an external form of worship to the various ways of life already in existence. He came down in human form to call mankind to a divine and heavenly life. He called us to radically change our own natures, to be born again of the Holy Spirit, to walk in the wisdom and light and love of God, to renounce the plausible ways of the world, and generally to become fit for an eternal, glorious enjoyment of God.

A single instance of the earthly or sensual in a Christian's life is a defiling spot; it ought to be washed out with tears of repentance. But a continuing habit of earthliness or sensuality is, in effect, a renouncement of our profession of faith.

CHAPTER TEN
JOY

SOME people will perhaps object that the rules for holy living restrain human life too much; that by considering God first in everything, we fill ourselves with anxiety. Further, some might argue that in depriving ourselves of so many seemingly innocent pleasures, we must be made perpetually downcast, bored, and gloomy.

I will answer those objections. These rules are intended not for a dull, anxious life, but for precisely the opposite. Instead of being anxious, we will become contented; we will exchange pursuit for fulfillment. Before taking on a holy life we cannot understand the solid enjoyments of a sound mind. In effect, our lower cravings have spoiled our taste for truly good things.

Imagine a person free from pride, envy, greed, lust, and other passions. Would not that person find real satisfaction? But take away one virtue from his life, replacing it with one vice, and by that degree his happiness will be reduced. All trouble and uneasiness comes from lacking something or other. Therefore, anything that increases our desires and supposed needs correspondingly increases our dissatisfaction.

God has sent us into the world with few physical needs—primarily food, drink, and shelter. Even if a person owned half the world, he would still have no further physical needs. The world is quite capable of supplying those needs. One would think that this by itself—a world created to fill man's needs—would certainly satisfy and content most people. But our passions fill our lives with imaginary lackings. Pride, envy, and ambition create desires as though God had created us with a thousand needs that cannot be satisfied.

Ask any downcast person why he is troubled. Almost certainly he will turn out to be the author of his own torment.

Celia is a fine example of vexation. She has an illness. It upsets her greatly, for she sees others who deserve disease far more. She blames God for "unjustly" allowing illness to such a fine person as herself.

If we could only infuse Celia with Christian humility, she would need nothing else to become a marvelously happy person. She would be grateful to God for any moments of improvement he chooses to allow, and be satisfied with her regular condition.

It is not Christianity that makes life anxious or uncomfortable, but the lack of it.

Many people believe a moderate dose of Christianity—not an excessive amount—will fulfill our lives. They believe vaulting ambition to be bad, but moderate ambition good. One might as well say that excessive pain hurts, but moderate pain feels good.

Another possible objection to rules for holy living is that so many things in this world are good. Created by God, they should be used; but following strict guidelines limits our enjoyment of them.

Suppose a person without knowledge of our world is placed alone with bread, wine, gold dust, iron chains, and gravel. He has no ability through his senses to use those items properly. Being thirsty, he puts wine in his ear. Hungry, he fills his mouth with gravel. Cold, he covers himself with chains. Tired, he sits on his bread. This person will vainly torment himself while he lives blinded with dust, choked with gravel, and burdened with chains.

Now suppose some benevolent being would come and instruct him in the proper use of those materials, warning him that other uses of those materials would be either profitless or harmful. Could anyone believe that those strict guidelines would make his life miserable?

In effect, Christianity teaches us how to properly use the world. It teaches us what is strictly right about food, drink, clothing, housing, employment, and other items. We learn to expect no more from them than they can properly provide.

The Scriptures tell us that although this world can satisfy physical needs, there is a much greater good prepared for mankind, reserved for us to enjoy when this short life is over. Christianity teaches that this state of glory awaits those who do not blind themselves with gold dust or eat gravel or load themselves with chains in their pain—in other words, those who use things rightly and reasonably.

If Christianity calls us to a life of prayer and watchfulness, it is only because we are surrounded by enemies and always in need of God's assistance. If we are to confess our sins, it is because such confessions relieve the mind and restore it to ease, just as weights taken off the shoulders relieve the body.

If prayer were not important, we would not be called to continue in it. When we consider that the other things we do are primarily or solely for the body, we should rejoice at prayer—it raises us above these poor concerns and opens our minds to heavenly things.

How ignorant people are to think that a life of strict devotion is dull and without comfort. It is plain that there is neither comfort nor joy to be found in anything else!

CHAPTER ELEVEN
THE MEASURE OF HAPPINESS

FELICIA is wealthy, attractive, and typical of her set. Ten years ago her favorite pleasures were television, records, nice clothes, cards, and light conversation. Her current enjoyments are the same, and ten years from now one would still expect no change. Felicia has never known a pleasant day in her life without at least one of these pleasures being available.

This happiness has deafened her to Christianity; she has been too cheerful to consider something as dull as eternity. It is for fear of losing some of this happiness that she dares not meditate on true joy.

Geneva is a devout but impoverished and unattractive maid. Suppose some woman would say, "I would rather be Geneva than Felicia." I would say that woman understood Christianity. Unfortunately, however, most Christian women expect the happiness of both Felicia and Geneva. In effect, to cite a Scriptural parallel, they want to be the rich man on earth and the beggar Lazarus in heaven.

It is easy to ridicule someone who sits hours every day in front of a television, vegetating through life. It is more difficult for us to see the waste in someone who maintains interest in a variety of clubs, entertainments, and activities. But think of it this way: a person who tries to quench his thirst by continually holding the same tarnished, empty cup to his lips is ignorant. But is it any less foolish for a person to hold a variety of empty golden cups to his lips? If all the world's activities are only so many empty cups, what does it matter which you take or how many you have?

Perhaps it is difficult for us to meditate on divine perfection or to contemplate the glories of heaven; after all, those are fairly advanced meditations. But anyone can contemplate the foolishness of pride or the uncertainty of life; these require no particular mental vigor. In fact, these meditations are taught us by almost everything we see and hear. This is the wisdom that life continually teaches us: there is no real happiness outside of Christianity.

CHAPTER TWELVE
MISERY OF LIFE

JESUS said, "Blessed are your eyes, for they see: and your ears, for they hear" (Matt. 13:16).

This verse teaches us two things. First, the dullness and heaviness of most people's minds regarding spiritual matters is so great that it can be compared to lacking eyes and ears. Second, God has so filled every life with arguments for godliness that people will certainly notice them if only they will properly use their eyes and ears.

What could be a greater motive to a Christian life than the fleetingness of earthly enjoyments? And who can help noticing this every day?

What greater call is there to look toward God than the pains, burdens, and vexations of life? And who does not feel this regularly?

What message from heaven could speak louder to us than the daily dying and departure of our fellow creatures? The great end of life is not left to be discovered by fine reasoning and deep reflections, but is pressed upon us in the plainest manner.

Let us simply intend to see and hear, and the whole world will become a book of wisdom. All disappointments and miseries will become as advice to us.

Imagine a man with tuberculosis or cancer. Suppose this man is wholly intent on doing everything in the spirit of Christianity, making wise use of his time, money, and abilities. He has no taste for gaudiness or extravagance, but seeks all his comfort in the hope of religion. We would certainly commend his prudence. We would say he has taken the right method to make himself as joyful as anyone can be in such a state.

On the other hand, if we should see the same person with trembling hands, short breath, and hollow eyes, intent upon business and bargaining as long as he can speak, and pleased by fine clothing when he can scarcely stand to be dressed, we would certainly condemn him as a foolish man.

It is easy to see the logic, wisdom, and happiness of a religious spirit in a cancer-stricken man. Pursuing the same line of thinking, however, we will easily see the same wisdom and happiness of being holy in every other state of life. For how soon everyone currently in good health will enter a state of weakness.

Some people believe that if they knew they only had one more year to live, they would stop worrying about reputation and finances; they would devote that year totally to God. At this moment, of course, any of us actually may have only one year left to live. But suppose someone has two years left to live. Couldn't he just as easily give two years to God as one?

If a person were told he only had five years left to live, he would realize this world was not a world for him. He would begin to prepare diligently for another world. Now who but a lunatic would assert that he knows he has even five years left?

It is said that a day to God is as a thousand years and a thousand years as a day because in his eternity, the passage of time is insignificant. We are created to be eternal, so it doesn't really matter whether our remaining time on earth is thirty years or thirty days.

Imagine three different types of rational beings. One type lives a week, another type lives a year, and the third a century. If these beings meet together and talk about time, they will have quite different understandings of it.

To make a true judgment of time, we must consider the true duration of our existence. If we are temporary beings, then a few years may justly be called a great deal; but if we are eternal beings, a few years are nothing. Most people believe their actions have temporary effects, several years at the very most. But when we come to truly believe that our actions have eternal repercussions, we will take each of them more seriously.

CHAPTER THIRTEEN
HOW TO PRAY

PRAYER is the nearest approach to God and the highest enjoyment of him we can experience in this life. When our hearts are full of God, sending up holy desires to the throne of grace, we can be no higher until death is swallowed up in glory.

On days when they do not have to work, some people spend the extra time in sleep rather than in prayer. This is a crime against Christianity. If we can rise at a certain hour for work, what does it say about our priorities that we cannot rise at that same hour for prayer?

If we consider devotion to be simply a certain amount of prayer time, we may perform it in spite of excess sleep. But if we consider it a state of the heart that desires the Spirit of God more than all other things, we will discover that prayer and self-indulgence cannot coexist. Self-denial is the soul of holiness. Whoever lacks even the self-denial to rise for prayer has no reason to think he has taken up his cross and is following Christ. What conquest has he had over himself, what trials is he prepared for, when he cannot rise for prayer at a time when the world rises for work?

As to the format for daily prayer, I think most Christians

ought to use specific forms or patterns. Each person should begin with a set topic; then if he finds his heart in the midst of prayer breaking forth into higher devotion, he can follow those fervors. Private devotion should be under the direction of a form but not tied down to it.

Sometimes our hearts are so full of sorrow for our sins that we cannot confess them in any language but tears. Sometimes God's light shines so clearly upon us and we are so affected by his love and goodness that our hearts worship and adore in a language higher than words; we feel transported by devotion.

On the other hand, sometimes we are so sunk into our bodies that our hearts are much too low for our prayers; we utter thanks and praises to God, but our hearts have little or no share in them. Thus it is necessary to be prepared for either occasion—form for the dull times and flexibility for the vibrant times.

The first thing you should do in prayer is to shut your eyes and in silence place your soul in the presence of God. Separate yourself from all common thoughts and make your heart sensitive to the divine presence. (How poorly we perform our devotions when we are in a hurry. We are saying prayers rather than praying.)

As often as possible, pray in the same place. If you reserve a room (or part of a room) for God, it will affect your thoughts; you will more readily enter a spirit of prayer.

When you begin your prayers, consider the attributes of God. Use names for him that express his wisdom and majesty. Names that express God's greatness raise our hearts into worship and adoration. Although prayer does not consist of fine phrases or studied expressions, words that speak highly of God raise the thoughts of the soul.

68

If you are asking Christ's spiritual assistance, remember his miracles. This will increase your faith in his power and goodness.

In reading Scripture and other Christian books, whenever you discover a passage that gives your heart a new motion toward God, you should try to give it a place in your prayers. In this way you will improve your prayers; you will be learning new ways of making your heart's desires known to God.

A good way to begin morning devotions is to offer all that you are and have to his service. Receive every day as a renewing of life; let your heart praise the glorious Creator. Feel free to add other thoughts as your emotions and circumstances move you; offering your circumstances to God sanctifies them.

Christians often seem bored, wondering about how to dispose of their time. They should give part of their time to prayer preparation, searching for helps to a devout spirit. If they would transcribe Scripture-prayers and gather praises and petitions from the Psalms, they could pray more meaningfully. If they meditated on these thoughts habitually, they could pray more deeply.

Why do most people benefit so little from prayer? It is because they do not consider devotion something to be nursed and cherished. But it needs to be continually improved with care and diligent use of methods and helps. Of course, Spirit-filled prayer is a gift from God, not attainable through our own power. However, it is generally given to those who prepare themselves for the reception of it.

Merle is an intelligent businessman, organized and efficient. He faithfully reads the business dailies and weeklies, keeps careful financial records, and generally increases his knowledge each year. The only thing he has not improved is his prayer life. He still uses the same thought level (and even the same words) that his mother heard him use when he was a child.

Merle never does any job, even raking the grass, without considering how to do it more effectively. But he has never considered how improvable is the spirit of devotion, how many helps a wise Christian may call to his assistance, and how necessary it is that our prayer should be enlarged and varied to reflect our lives. If Merle sees a book on prayer, he passes it by just as he would a Dick-and-Jane reader; he assumes he sufficiently learned both to pray and to read as a child.

How pitiable is this man's conduct!

Or consider Kevin, a successful dentist. He thinks that by refusing to read any other Christian book except the Bible that he exalts the Bible's status.

It is very well, Kevin, to prefer the Bible to all other books. But if you will read only the Bible because it is the best, why do you not follow this practice in your dentistry? Why do you not limit yourself to a single drill—the best?

In dentistry, Kevin searches out tools for every possible situation. In prayer, however, he thinks one tool sufficient. Devotion is right understanding of God; right affection for God. All practices, then, that heighten our comprehension of God are means of devotion. They nourish and fix our affections on him.

CHAPTER FOURTEEN
PRAY WITH GRATITUDE

BEGIN your prayers with a psalm. I suggest that you not simply read the psalm, but chant or sing it. This will call your spirit to its proper duty and tune your soul to worship and adoration.

Psalms create a sense of delight in God. They awaken holy desires and teach you how to ask. They turn your heart into an altar.

In all states of mind, our inward emotions produce suitable outward actions. These outward actions then tend to increase the inward emotions. For example, just as anger produces angry words, angry words increase anger. Likewise, chanting or singing psalms (the outward action) increases delight in God (the inner emotion). Souls and bodies have a mutual power of acting on one another.

I encourage this practice because it develops thankfulness. There is no state of mind as holy and excellent as thankfulness to God. Consequently, nothing is more important than exercising and developing this mind-set.

A dull, complaining spirit—often characteristic of Christians—is of all attitudes the one most contrary to Christianity. It disowns the God it pretends to adore. To not adore God as infinitely good is, in effect, to disown him.

For a person must believe that the world's events are guided by the care of a Being who is all love and goodness to his creatures. If a person does not believe this, he can hardly be said to believe in God. But if a person believes that everything that happens to him is for the best, then he cannot complain about wanting something better. A complaint is an accusation that God has failed to be sufficiently good. Thankfulness is an acknowledgement of his goodness.

The greatest saint is not the person who prays most, fasts most, or gives most to charity. It is the one who wills everything as God wills, who receives everything as an instance of God's goodness. All prayer, repentance, and meditation are simply ways of conforming our souls to God, of filling ourselves with thankfulness and praise for everything that comes from God.

The shortest, surest way to happiness is to thank and praise God for everything that happens. If you thank and praise God for whatever calamity, you turn it into a blessing.

Therefore, it is a good idea to sing praises to God during your prayers. Some might object that this is like making our prayers public, doing them to be heard by others. But the privacy of prayer is not destroyed by having witnesses— only by seeking witnesses. Remember the Scriptural example of Paul and Silas, who sang psalms of praise while in prison, with the other prisoners listening to them.

Psalms 34, 96, 103, 111, 146, and 147 particularly set forth the glory of God. You may choose instead to take the finest parts of several different psalms and piece them together. Do whatever is fitting for your own devotion.

CHAPTER FIFTEEN
PRAY FOR HUMILITY

YOUR devotional life is not evaluated simply on how often you pray. Yet imagine yourself placed somewhere in the air, a spectator of all that passes in the world. You observe, in one view, the prayers that all Christians offer to God each day. Some Christians are constantly calling upon God, inviting him into their lives regularly. Others pray rarely, only at especially convenient times.

Now if you were to see this as God sees it, how do you think you would be affected by the sight? Could you really believe that those who pray haphazardly receive the same benefits from prayer as those who pray regularly? Which group of people do you think most readily perceives itself as servants or slaves of God?

Scripture exhorts frequent prayer almost as strongly as prayer at all. We can be sure that those who pray frequently are receiving the real blessings of prayer. Furthermore, frequent prayer is an effective way of adding virtue to your life. Suppose a materialistic man were to pray every day regarding his materialism. He would pray through temptations as they arose and ask God's assistance in rejecting them all. Eventually he would find his conscience so much awakened that he could no longer earnestly pray that way without changing his life.

If you are considering what virtue to begin praying for, I recommend humility. It may be the least intended virtue among Christians. And since every good thought or action lays us open to pride, a person advancing in other virtues may actually be receding in humility.

Humility does not mean having a lower opinion of ourselves than we deserve, but having a just sense of our weakness and sin. We are too weak of ourselves to do anything, even exist. It is solely the power of God which allows us to do anything, including moving toward him. Thus pride is like theft; the proud take God's glory to themselves.

To develop personal humility during your meditations, simply examine your life. Suppose that all of your thoughts would suddenly be transparent to the world. If everyone knew what secret motivations corrupt even your most noble actions, you would no longer expect to be respected for your goodness.

Think how shameful the nature of sin is, how great the atonement necessary to cleanse us of its guilt. Nothing less was required than the suffering and death of the Son of God. Is there any room for pride while we partake in such a nature as this?

All of us love humility and hate pride—in other people.

Turn your eyes toward heaven and consider how different you are from the angels. They do not contemplate their perfections, but they all have the same joy. Consider how unreasonable it is for human sinners to bask in their positions of respect while the magnificent seraphim give honor to God alone. Let a person who is pleased with himself contemplate our blessed Lord nailed and stretched out upon a cross, comparing himself to that meek and crucified Savior.

CHAPTER SIXTEEN
OUR CRUCIFIXION

IN striving for humility, we must consider ourselves learners. We have to learn something contrary to our former habits of mind. We must lay aside our own spirit of self-centeredness.

We are born in pride, which stems naturally from our self-love. This is one reason Christianity is so often represented as a new birth and a new spirit. Gospel history is the history of Christ's conquest over the spirit of the world. True Christians are those who, following the spirit of Christ, have lived contrary to the spirit of the world.

"If any man have not the Spirit of Christ, he is none of his" (Rom. 8:9). "Set your affection on things above, not on things of the earth. For ye are dead, and your life is hid with Christ in God" (Col. 3:2, 3). This is the language of the whole New Testament; this is the mark of Christianity. We are to be dead (to the spirit of the world) and live a new life in the spirit of Jesus Christ. But in spite of the clarity of these doctrines, many Christians live and die slaves to the customs of the world.

Our conquest of the world is pictured in the crucifixion. Christianity implies an absolute conformity to the spirit Christ showed in his self-sacrifice on the cross.

It was this Christlike spirit that made Paul so passionately express himself in Galatians 6:14: "God forbid that I should glory, save in the cross of our Lord Jesus Christ." But why did Paul glory "in the cross"? Is it because Christ had suffered in his place and excused him from suffering? Not at all. It was because his Christian profession of faith had called him to the honor of suffering with Christ, and of dying to the world under reproach, even as Christ did on the cross. Paul immediately adds, ". . . by [him] the world is crucified unto me, and I unto the world."

For that reason the cross of Christ was the glory of Christians in Paul's day. It didn't just show their willingness to acknowledge a crucified Master. It showed that they gloried in a religion that was completely dependent upon a doctrine of crucifixion. It called them to the same self-sacrifice, the same meekness and humility, the same patient bearing of reproach, and the same dying to this world's happiness, that Christ showed on the cross.

To have a true idea of Christianity, we should not consider that Christ simply suffered in our places, but that his special merit makes our suffering acceptable to God when joined with his. Without Christ's sacrifice, our self-sacrifices would not be fit for God. And the opposite is equally true: unless we are crucified and risen with Christ, his crucifixion and resurrection profit us nothing.

The whole tenor of Scripture points out this connection between Christ and us: "If we suffer, we shall also reign with him" (2 Tim. 2:12); "Our old man is crucified with him" (Rom. 6:6); "If we be dead with him, we shall also live with him" (2 Tim. 2:11); "If ye then be risen with Christ, seek those things which are above" (Col. 3:1). In all things, then, our lives are "hid with Christ in God" (Col. 3:3). Thus an individual's salvation obviously depends on his personal death and resurrection joined with Christ's.

Since the spirit of the world nailed our Lord to the cross, everyone who has the spirit of Christ—who opposes the world as he did—will be crucified one way or another. After all, Christianity still lives in the same world.

"Because ye are not of the world," our Lord said, "the world hateth you" (John 15:19). We are apt to lose the meaning of these words because we tend to think they were meant exclusively for the disciples. But Jesus did not add, as a way of consolation, that at some time the world would cease to hate his followers.

You may perhaps doubt the relevance of Christ's statement for us today, saying that the world (or at least the part where we live) has now become Christian. Surely, however, you would not claim that most people in "Christian" countries have the spirit of Christ. And the world's profession of Christianity makes it an even more dangerous enemy than before. The favors, riches, and enjoyments of the world have swayed far more Christians than its persecutions ever did. Since the world no longer seems an enemy, more Christians are content to be directed by it.

How many consciences are kept quiet simply because their sins are never condemned by the church? How many individuals ignore New Testament directives because the Christian world does? How many of us would have the audacity to live our lives so contrary to primitive Christianity if it were not that the other people in the church live the same way? There is nothing that a good Christian ought to guard against more constantly than the authority of the Christian world.

CHAPTER
SEVENTEEN
PRIDE AND
EDUCATION

ONE would suppose that Christian elementary and secondary schools, Bible colleges, and seminaries would teach young people to begin their lives in a spirit of Christianity. But such is not the case. Pride is the primary motivating factor we try to awaken in children and young adults. We do everything we can to puff up their minds with a sense of their own abilities. We exhort them to everything from corrupt motives. We stir them to try to excel others and to shine in the eyes of the world.

We thrust these motives on them until they believe it dutiful to be proud of their accomplishments. And when we have taught them to seek distinction, then we promise the world they will "amount to something."

If young people are in seminary studying for the ministry, we set before them some eminent orator whose fine preaching has made him famous. We encourage them to desire this type of honor.

Of course, the same is true of young adults outside seminaries. If they seem interested in becoming lawyers, we encourage them by telling them how much money a lawyer makes.

87

And after all this, we wonder why children and young adults grow older so full of pride, ambition, and envy. But if we teach a child to thirst for applause, is it any wonder that he will continue to do so the rest of his life?

Some might object to my line of reason, and argue that we bring famous speakers into seminaries so that students can imitate their speaking techniques, not so students will be impressed with their credentials. I can only reply that I never hear this distinction stressed. Further, I think it difficult to separate the lecturer's speaking ability from his fame.

One might argue that we need the spur of glorification to make young people industrious. One could as easily argue that older adults need glorification to make them industrious. And that is, in fact, just what we have: a population of very industrious adults without humility.

As Christians, we can remove the desire to be on top, to beat the competition, and not have the young grow lazy. Can anyone imagine that children educated by Christ or the apostles would have been idle? On the contrary, Jesus performed countless worthy and glorious actions while displaying a profound humility.

How then should we teach our children to view education? A certain Christian's conversation with his son illustrates a healthy approach:

"Son, I love you. But you are under the care of a much greater Father than I, whose love is far greater than mine.

"First of all, then, worship and adore God; think of him magnificently, speak of him reverently, adore his power, continue in his service, and pray to him constantly.

"Next to this, love your neighbor—all mankind—as affectionately as you love yourself. Think how God loves all, how merciful he is to them, how carefully he preserves them. Then strive to love the world's people as God does.

"Son, I'd like to give you some advice about school. If you

enjoy outdoing your classmates, you will want to see them do things less well. This is not right. Be as glad to see wisdom and intelligence in other people, then, as in yourself. God is as pleased to see other people learn as to see you learn. 'It pleases God'—let this be your only motive for good work.

"I want you to learn history, not because I particularly want you to be a professional historian, but so that at proper times you may look into the history of past ages and learn the methods of God's providence. Reading the writings of the wise, you may fortify your mind with their sayings.

"Fill your heart with love for God and your neighbor. Go no deeper as a scholar than these loves will bear.

"Have no ambition conflicting with your personal purity and perfection. Live in such a way that you can be glad God is present everywhere, aware of all your actions. Don't desire to put down your equals, and don't grow bitter at those who try to get ahead of you. Your humility probably won't do others any good, but it certainly is a good thing for you.

"There is one person, though, with whom you are always in competition, one whom you should continually strive to exceed in excellence—yourself."

CHAPTER EIGHTEEN
FEMALE EDUCATION

A CHRISTIAN orientation is as important for girls as for boys. Tragically, however, girls have not only been traditionally educated in pride, but usually in the silliest forms of it.

We seldom encourage them to compete with boys in the sciences and in public speaking (where I suspect they would often prove superior). Rather, we turn them over to the study of beauty and dress. Indeed, the whole world conspires to make them think of little else. Fathers, mothers, friends, and relatives all have the same well-meaning wishes for a girl: may she have a pretty face, a fine figure, and fashionable clothes.

I believe that a woman's first step to humility would be to forget whatever she has been taught to desire. Generally speaking, even good parents primarily recognize and compliment their daughters in nonspiritual areas.

Society's treatment of women is a particular tragedy because in most areas they have such a clear understanding of Christianity. Christian women regularly exceed Christian men in holiness.

It's often said that women are naturally vain. That's as unreasonable as saying that Jews are naturally stingy. Expectations and conditioning generally make them a certain way, not their natures. Popular magazines, television shows, movies, and advertisements often picture women simply as painted dolls, as frivolous creatures made to gratify men's passions.

Whenever a woman is complimented on something for which men generally are not recognized, she should consider that she is being betrayed away from perfection. Friends to her vanity are not friends. Women should remember that they live for God, not others; their reasoning ability is as great as men's, and they have not only the right but the responsibility to seek wisdom as fervently as men should.

We often accuse women of being too ready to accept the first handsome, pleasant man to come along. It's no wonder that they should like in men what they have been taught to admire in themselves.

How then should young women be brought up? Evelyn furnishes an example. She has two daughters, but never looks at them simply in that way. They are her spiritual children, and she is their spiritual mother.

Evelyn teaches them to do all kinds of work, both domestic and mechanical. "I want you to always be of service to others, whether you are rich or poor," she says to them.

Since society pressures women to be primarily concerned with their bodies, Evelyn strives to counteract that attitude. "My children," she says, "I want you to know yourselves. Though you have bodies, you are more than that; you are spirits. You are made in God's image for eternity. Everything physical about you is like clothing—something to be used appropriately for awhile, but which is wearing away.

"Always keep in mind these two beings inside you. Your permanent part desires purity; your temporary part inclines toward pleasure. You often feel this internal war, don't you? And you know by reasoning that the permanent part is clearly more important. But movies, television shows, commercials, and popular magazines would certainly not teach you this.

"Considering your bodies as residences, keep them pure and clean. Considering your bodies as servants, give them enough food, rest, and clothing to perform their duties.

"If you give your bodies more attention than this or your souls less, you are unwise. In fact, a person more intent on adorning her body than perfecting her soul is as foolish as a person who would prefer nice clothes to good health. In short, cultivate your mind more than your body.

"As to whether you get married or remain single, I do not worry about that, and neither should you. Never consider yourself simply a person to be admired and courted by men. Live for your own sake, for God.

"Regarding handicrafts, I have not taught you those skills simply for amusement, as an activity to while away the hours. When you were little I left you to little amusements, but now you know God and yourselves. You know the worth of employing yourselves for God. So turn your handiwork into gifts for others, particularly the less fortunate, and your skills will be changed from busywork to holy service.

"Love those people most who most turn you toward God.

"Though you intend to marry, yet do not until you find a man laboring toward the same perfections you are—someone who will be a friend to your virtues, someone whose constant example will benefit you.

"Strive to do praiseworthy things, but do nothing in order to be praised. Don't expect a reward from others for right living. And above all, don't be proud of your own virtues. As soon as people start living differently from the world, Satan points out to them how wonderful they are for doing so. He is quite content that people do a good work if they will only be proud of it.

"Never allow yourselves, therefore, to look down on those who do not possess as many Christian virtues as you. Force yourselves to love them, and pray to God for them. Let humility whisper that you would have lost those virtues if God had left you to your own strength and wisdom."

CHAPTER NINETEEN
LOVE AND INTERCESSORY PRAYER

I HAVE spoken earlier about prayers of gratitude and prayers for spiritual growth. Now I will speak of intercessory prayer—prayer for others. Our Lord recommended his love for us as a pattern of our love for each other. Since he continually makes intercession for us all, we ought to pray for each other.

Christ said, "A new commandment I give unto you, That ye love one another; as I have loved you" (1 John 13:34). It certainly wasn't a new commandment for people to love each other; this had clearly been taught in the law of Moses. But its newness lay in its imitation of a new example— we are to love one another as Christ has loved us.

There is nothing in us more acceptable to God than our love for others, our wishing and praying for their happiness. Nothing else makes us more like God, the very source of love. But love unites us to God only when it imitates the love God shows to his creatures.

God wills happiness to all beings, even though nothing can increase his own unbounded happiness. Therefore we must desire happiness for others even when it doesn't create any happiness for us.

God delights in his people becoming more perfect; therefore we should rejoice in it. God is willing to forgive everyone; we should be equally willing to forgive. And God has given us all an equally accessible source of happiness (himself), so that we would have no reason to envy or despise one another. We cannot possibly rival one another in God's happiness. And as for temporal, material things, they are so foreign to our real happiness that they should be no occasion for spite.

Regarding intercessory prayer, our external acts of love are limited by time, money, and energy. We cannot contribute physical relief to more than a few people. But through prayer we have infinite power. God attributes to us the acts of love that we would perform if we could.

We cannot care for all the sick, relieve all the poor, or comfort all of those in distress. We *can* pray for them, however, and God will consider us their benefactors. We cannot care for every elderly Christian; but if we thank God for those who do, we will be received by God as a sharer in that ministry.

A man who lusts after a woman is considered an adulterer, even though he has only performed the act in his mind. A person who longingly prays blessings for those beyond his reach is therefore considered a benefactor, even though he has only helped them in his mind.

Just as the sins of the world made the Son of God become a compassionate offering for all mankind, so no one of Christ's spirit can be without compassion for sinners. There is no greater sign of our own perfecting than when we love those who are weak and defective. All sin, of course, is to be hated wherever it is; but we must set ourselves against sin as we do against sickness: by being compassionate toward the sick. All hatred of sin must fill the heart with sorrow toward the person miserably mired in it.

Some Christians often think that if they can't bear being around horrid people, that proves their love of virtue. But if this had been the spirit of Jesus Christ, if he had hated sinners in this way, there would have been no redemption of the world. The higher our sense of virtue, the more we will want to rescue those without it.

Why do we love others? Because they are wise, holy, and virtuous? No, for often they are not. We love others to imitate and obey God. God loves us in order to make us good; this then, must be the pattern of our love for others.

Perhaps you will ask, "How is it possible to love a bad man as much as a good man?" It happens in the same way it's possible to be truthful to a bad man. You do not determine how truthful you will be by how good the other person is, do you? You know that truth is founded in God's nature, not in people's merits. The same is true of love.

Perhaps you will further ask, "Aren't we supposed to esteem and honor good men?" Certainly! But esteem and honor are different from love. Love makes you want another's utmost happiness; esteem makes you desire to be like another.

Constantly consider how you love yourself as a measure of your love for others. You know how unpleasant it is to do something foolish or to have your weaknesses known. Therefore, if you enjoy telling about others' foolishness or exposing their weaknesses, or listening to their weaknesses and foolishness being exposed, you do not truly love them. On the contrary, those are acts of hate.

If, as Paul says, the lack of love is such a great shortcoming that it renders our greatest virtues as empty sounds, we desperately need to study the art of love. I therefore implore you to seek love regularly when you pray.

CHAPTER TWENTY
INTERCESSION AND MUTUAL SUPPORT

IN his epistles, Paul tells churches and individual Christians that they are the constant subject of his prayers. He writes to the Philippians, "I thank my God upon every remembrance of you" (Phil. 1:3). To Timothy he writes, "I thank God . . . that without ceasing I have remembrance of thee in my prayers night and day" (2 Tim. 1:3). The ancient Christians did not cement their hearts with human interests but with mutual communication of spiritual blessings, with prayers and thanksgivings to God for each other. Christians used to astound the world with their love for one another.

Pray for others, then, as long and earnestly as you pray for yourself. You will find your heart growing generous, delighting in others' happiness instead of just your own. If you beg God to make someone eternally happy, you will want to see steps taken toward that on earth. It would be strange to ask God to make a sick person well but not to care whether he gets the necessary medicine.

Though we are to treat all Christians as brothers, we can live in the society of only a few; therefore we should particularly intercede for those with whom we have contact. If you are kind in your prayers to those around you, it will be much easier to treat your neighbors kindly. Nothing can make us love a person more than praying for him. You will find it easy to forgive those whom you are asking God to forgive. These prayers teach Christians to consider each other as members of a spiritual family, fellow-heirs of future glory.

Oliver is the minister of a small congregation. He loves his people and prays for them as often as he prays for himself. He tries to know everyone's way of life and spiritual state so he can pray for them wisely.

When he first served the congregation, rudeness or cantankerousness on anyone's part would drive Oliver wild; now it raises in him a desire to pray. It is delightful to see how vigorously he instructs and how firmly yet tenderly he reproves; he has first prayed for those he instructs and reproves.

Oliver has been greatly affected by James 5:16: "The effectual fervent prayer of a righteous person availeth much." He reads how God said of Job, "My servant Job shall pray for you: for him I will accept" (Job 42:8).

From these passages Oliver concludes that extra-holy people have extraordinary power with God. This makes Oliver even more studious of Christian perfection, not wishing to hinder his prayers.

Parents should make themselves intercessors for their children. I suppose most Christian parents ask God to "bless" their children in a general way; but I'm speaking of prayer for specific spiritual needs. It would cause parents to be very careful of everything they said or did, not wanting their example to hinder their prayers.

How can people most readily perfect their hearts? By interceding with God for those who irritate or frustrate them. Suppose that you have a misunderstanding with a friend, neighbor, or relative. If you will ask God to give them every blessing and happiness you can think of, you will have taken the speediest way of setting your heart back on its Christian course. Great resentments between friends often arise from minor incidents; mutual prayer relieves the ill temper.

Intercessory prayer can reveal our true feelings to us. Steven was a good Christian with one serious fault: he loved to hear and tell the defects of everyone in the church. When he visited, you generally heard him say how sorry he was that Mrs. X had certain failings, which he proceeded to describe. He related the most uncharitable stories so tenderly that most listeners felt he showed true Christian concern.

Once Steven told a friend of another person's weakness, a weakness too shameful to be mentioned in public. He ended by saying how glad he was that the information was not publicly known.

His friend replied, "Steven, you say you are glad, for this person's sake, that his weakness is not yet well-known. Go home, then, and pray to God for this man. Pray as earnestly as you would if you were the one hoping to save your reputation. Beg God to save him. Implore God to rescue him from those who are spreading his shame with secret stories. When you have fervently prayed this, then you may, if you wish, tell another friend what you have just told me."

Steven was greatly affected by this rebuke. From then till now he has constantly interceded, and it has changed his heart. Now Steven would no more tell a story to reveal someone's weakness than he would pray to God to harm that person.

CHAPTER
TWENTY-ONE
SELF-EXAMINATION

SELF-EXAMINATION is a most helpful type of prayer. Scripture says, "If we confess our sins, he is faithful and just to forgive us our sins, and to cleanse us from all unrighteousness" (1 John 1:9). This verse implies that if we ignore or hold back our sins, we cannot expect to be forgiven. And, obviously, a person cannot confess sins if he hasn't looked for them.

Perhaps you simply confess yourself a sinner in general and ask forgiveness for your sins in a lump sum. That is as unreasonable as telling a grocer you want nothing specific, just food in general.

What is confession supposed to do, after all? For one thing, it should make you ashamed of your sins. Surely remembering particular sins will bring about a greater sorrow than generalization. True confession should be truly useful.

For instance, suppose that one day you were to exaggerate during a conversation to make yourself look better. If you were to recall the transgression, condemn yourself before God, beg his pardon, and ask the assistance of his grace against that sin in the future, what could give you greater help against it? If you should commit that sin the next day and go through the process again, the emotional pain and remorse would make you even more desirous of perfection. In cases of repeated sin, we would certainly see ourselves humbled and eventually changed. But a formal, general confession has little or no effect on the mind.

To make prayerful examination even more beneficial, a person should most closely and regularly examine the areas in which he has traditionally had most difficulty. For example, a person who knows that he has trouble with anger should consider every thought, word, and action for evidence of this passion.

A person should also examine his regular routine. Does the way he work or eat glorify God? These examinations will give a person newness of mind, desire for perfection, and wisdom of spirit such as he has never had before.

Always try to remember how odious sin is to God. Sin is a greater blemish to the soul than any filth or disease is to the body.

How easily God can create beings, we learn from the first chapter of Genesis. How difficult it is for infinite mercy to forgive sins, we learn from the bloody sacrifices, the costly atonement, and human deaths. God made the world by speaking, but he redeemed it by great labor. Because of sin, the Son of God was forced to become man, undergo a painful life, and be nailed to a cross. The bloody sacrifices of the Jewish law represent God's displeasure at sin. And the world is still under the curse of sin, with famines, disease, and tempests.

Consider all the sacrifices and sufferings, both of God and man, caused by sin. This will teach you with what sorrow you should purge yourself of it. To consider how thoroughly you should repent, imagine what level of repentance you would expect from the greatest sinner in the world.

The greatest saints of all ages have indeed condemned themselves as the greatest sinners, a position toward which such examination will move you. There are many things you know yourself to be guilty of that you cannot be sure about in others.

To properly sense your own sins, do not compare your life with other people's lives. You may indeed have less outward sin than they do. But to know your own guilt, consider your own advantages. You are educated, you have opportunities to read good books, you have known people whose lives served as fine examples. God may know people who have made less use of their advantages, but you cannot; you must know more of the benefits available to you than to others.

When you see how a certain person breaks God's laws, suppose you had been in his circumstances. You might have broken more!

CHAPTER
TWENTY-TWO
THE HIGHEST WISDOM

I HAVE explained devotion as both prayer and the consecrated life. One would think that Christians would naturally seek devotion. Experience, however, clearly shows that nothing has to be more repeatedly pressed upon our minds.

A person who practices devotion is master of the most excellent knowledge. And what could be better than to know the true worth of things?

If a person had eyes that could see beyond the stars but could not see anything close enough to be of practical use to him, we would reckon his vision very bad. In the same manner, if a person has a sharp wit and retentive memory but doesn't understand his relationship to God, he lacks useful understanding.

A man is considered a fool not because he lacks the five senses, but because he doesn't understand the proportionate worth of things. Undeniably, then, the person with a low IQ who seeks God wholeheartedly is wise; and the Ph.D. who ignores God is a fool.

The highest understanding is to rightly know our Creator. The wisest judgment is to live as if in his very presence.